Roberto Clemente

JUNIOR ▪ WORLD ▪ BIOGRAPHIES

A JUNIOR *HISPANICS OF ACHIEVEMENT* BOOK

Roberto Clemente

NORMAN L. MACHT

CHELSEA JUNIORS

a division of CHELSEA HOUSE PUBLISHERS

FRONTISPIECE: *The first Hispanic player to be elected to the Baseball Hall of Fame, Roberto Clemente was one of the greatest athletes in the history of the sport.*

English-language words that are italicized in the text can be found in the glossary at the back of the book.

Chelsea House Publishers

EDITORIAL DIRECTOR Richard Rennert
EXECUTIVE MANAGING EDITOR Karyn Gullen Browne
COPY CHIEF Robin James
PICTURE EDITOR Adrian G. Allen
ART DIRECTOR Robert Mitchell
MANUFACTURING DIRECTOR Gerald Levine
PRODUCTION COORDINATOR Marie Claire Cebrián-Ume

JUNIOR WORLD BIOGRAPHIES

SENIOR EDITOR Ann-Jeanette Campbell
SERIES DESIGN Marjorie Zaum

Staff for ROBERTO CLEMENTE
ASSOCIATE EDITOR David Shirley
EDITORIAL ASSISTANT Kelsey Goss
PICTURE RESEARCHER Sandy Jones
COVER ILLUSTRATION Dan O'Leary

First Printing

1 3 5 7 9 8 6 4 2

Library of Congress Cataloging-in-Publication Data
Macht, Norman L. (Norman Lee), 1929–
    Roberto Clemente / Norman L. Macht
      p. cm.—(Junior world biographies)
    Includes bibliographical references (p.) and index.
ISBN 0-7910-1764-8.
      0-7910-2541-1 (pbk.)
    1. Clemente, Roberto, 1934–1972—Juvenile literature. 2. Baseball players—United States—Biography—Juvenile literature. I. Title. II. Series.
GV865.C45M33 1994   93-26178
                                                                     CIP
                                                                     AC

1

Determined
To Be the Best

When the Pittsburgh Pirates prepared to confront the Baltimore Orioles in the 1971 World Series, Pirates right fielder Roberto Clemente was determined to be the star.

Every major league player dreams of playing in a World Series, but Clemente had even more at stake. He had been in the 1960 World Series, when the *underdog* Pirates defeated the mighty New York Yankees in seven games. Although Roberto hit safely in every game of that Series, his achievements had been overshadowed by the heroics of his teammate Bill Mazeroski. Mazeroski's dramatic ninth-inning home run had won the world championship game. In the delirious celebration that followed the Pirates' victory, few people remembered Clemente's exceptional performance on the field and at the plate. This year, however, Roberto was determined that things would be different.

Clemente had known triumphs during his illustrious career: National League Most Valuable Player in 1966, four batting titles, and 12 Gold Glove Awards during his 17 years in Pittsburgh. Yet he felt that he had never been given the recognition that he deserved. During those same years, other outfielders, such as Willie Mays and Mickey Mantle, seemed to get all the good publicity and top ratings.

Mays and Mantle were great players in their own right, and they hit many more home runs than Clemente. But the biggest difference was that Mantle and Mays played in New York and San

Francisco, two of the largest cities in the league. Sluggers in the larger cities had many more fans to sing their praises, and much greater newspaper and television coverage. Pittsburgh, a medium-sized industrial city in the southwest corner of Pennsylvania, was one of the smallest metropolitan areas in baseball.

There was also the issue of Clemente's Hispanic heritage. Roberto came from Puerto Rico, and although he was as much an American as other players in the league, he was still looked on as a foreigner by many players, writers, and fans. Black players had been in the big leagues since 1947, when the Brooklyn Dodgers' Jackie Robinson first broke the major league color barrier. But Clemente was the first outstanding player from Puerto Rico, where Spanish was the native language and the life and customs were different from the mainland.

Some of Clemente's problems, especially with the media, came from his honesty and outspokenness. Hampered by chronic aches and pains throughout his career, he simply told the truth whenever anyone asked him how he felt. "My neck, it hurts so bad," he would groan to a teammate or reporter. "My shoulder is so sore, and my back really aches."

"When you asked Roberto how he felt," recalled St. Louis Cardinals manager Joe Torre, "he always said, 'Not so good.' He had an ache or a pain here or there or somewhere else or in two places. Then he would go out and beat you with his bat or by taking hits away from you with great catches and maybe throw out a runner or two at home plate."

The newspapers called Roberto a complainer and a hypochondriac (one who suffers from imaginary ailments). If he sat out a game, he was accused of being lazy, or "jaking," as the players called it. By the time he had finished his career at Pittsburgh, however, Clemente had played more games than anyone who ever wore a Pirates uniform.

Some sportswriters and broadcasters called him a hot dog, or a show-off, because he always played so intensely and spectacularly, even when the Pirates were losing. Because of his all-out style of play, Clemente often looked good even when his teammates did not. Like fans everywhere, Pittsburgh fans believed what they read and heard in the media, and sometimes booed Roberto, even when he was playing well.

Through it all, Clemente knew that he was as great an outfielder as any in the game, and he did not hesitate to say so himself. He was very proud, and it constantly bothered him to be so unjustly criticized and underrated.

Prior to 1971, all World Series games had been played in the afternoon. Although the games had been televised for many years, most people had to work during the day and could not watch. This would be the first time that a World Series game would be played at night, and the audience would be much larger. Clemente was now 37 years old, an age at which most major league players had long since retired. He knew that this might be his last chance to perform in an important game where so many people could see how great a player he really was.

As the defending world champions, the Baltimore Orioles were big favorites to win the Series. Four of the team's pitchers had won 20 games each, which was only the second time that a team could boast of that accomplishment. The Orioles also had the big bats of future Hall of Famers Frank and Brooks Robinson. The Pirates could not match Baltimore's phenomenal pitching records, but they did have some sluggers of their own, including Clemente and Willie Stargell, who led the National League with 48 home runs.

The Orioles won the first two games in Baltimore, 5–3 and 11–3, but Clemente put on a show for the fans in the losing efforts for Pittsburgh. As usual, he was a terror with the bat, collecting two hits in each game. But it was his throwing arm, ranked by other players as the best in the business, that brought the crowd to its feet in the second game.

During a six-run fifth inning that broke open the game, the Orioles had a man on second base when Frank Robinson drove a long fly ball to deep right field. The runner tagged up at second and set off for third. Clemente sped back to the wall, made the catch, spun around, and threw a perfect *strike* to third base without a bounce. The runner barely beat the throw. But nobody in the ballpark had expected a throw at all, and everyone was astounded by how close the play had been. At once, the capacity crowd rose to its feet and cheered. From the dugout, the Baltimore players stared in disbelief, awed by the greatest throw they had ever seen.

The Series then moved to Pittsburgh, where Clemente gained even more respect as he led the Pirates to victory with sheer hustle and drive. Twice he beat throws to first base on easy infield rollers, driving in one run and scoring another in a 5–1 win.

Game four was the first World Series night game, and it drew a record television audience for a sporting event. This was what Roberto had been waiting for, the biggest stage of his life. Early in the game, Roberto hit a long drive down the right field foul line that looked like a certain home run. But the ball tailed off at the last moment, and the umpire called it a foul. Roberto was so wound up that he kept right on charging down the line. For five minutes, he argued furiously that it was a home run. Finally, when he was satisfied that the call would not be changed, he picked up his bat again and rapped out a base hit. He later added two more hits in the Pirates 4–3 win.

Roberto's fiery play ignited the entire Pittsburgh team to play their best ball of the season. The next day, the Pirates won their third straight game over the Orioles, 4–0.

Back in Baltimore for game six, Clemente continued to play like a one-man wrecking crew. Angered by a newspaper story that knocked his hitting ability and lack of power, Clemente tripled off the wall in the first inning and blasted a long home run in the third. It seemed that he could not do enough to prove how good he was. He played as if to say to the world, "Take that!" and "Now what do you think of the great Roberto?"

Late in the game with the Pirates in the field, Clemente prevented a tie-breaking Orioles run from scoring with a blistering throw to home plate. Some said it was even greater than his throw to third in game two. In spite of Roberto's heroics, the Orioles scored the game-winning run in the tenth inning to tie the Series.

In the deciding game, Clemente hit another home run and the underdog Pirates hung on to win 2–0. There was no doubt that Clemente was the Series' Most Valuable Player. He had batted .414 with 12 hits and had now hit safely in all 14 World Series games in which he had played. More important, Roberto had done what he had set out to do at the start of the Series. He had been determined to prove that he was the best player in the world, and the world, at last, had been convinced.

Clemente connects for a key hit in the fourth inning of the seventh and final game of the 1971 World Series.

Roberto had two more items on his *agenda* before he left the ballpark that last day of the Series. He wanted everybody to know that this was no special Clemente they had been watching, no one-week show-off playing beyond his true ability. "No big deal," he told a radio interviewer after the game. "I play like that all the time. All season. Every season."

Clemente's other message was delivered on television to his parents, who were watching from the home that he had bought for them in San Juan. As he accepted his Most Valuable Player trophy, Roberto said quietly, "First, I want to say something in Spanish to my mother and father. *En este, el momento más grande de mi vida, les pido la benedición.* (At this, the greatest moment of my life, I ask your blessing.)"

The village of Carolina, Puerto Rico, where Roberto grew up, probably looked much like the one pictured here: crowded, run-down, and poverty-stricken.

2

Born To
Play Ball

Roberto Walker Clemente was born on August 18, 1934, in Carolina, a small town on the Caribbean island of Puerto Rico. He was the youngest of seven children, including a boy and girl from his mother's previous marriage.

The family lived in a barrio (the Spanish word for neighborhood) of small wood-frame houses with zinc roofs, packed close together with tiny patches of dirt around them. The area where Roberto lived was surrounded by sugarcane fields, where most of the men worked. Cane grows straight as bamboo, taller than the ceiling of a classroom, and in dense bunches. When harvested, the sugarcane is cut close to the ground with a long, sharp knife called a machete, leaving behind hard, sharp stubs in the field. Then the cane's sticky juice is squeezed from it to make molasses and sugar. It takes many months of hard work to harvest sugarcane, and in Puerto Rico, where the weather is always hot, the burning sun saps the strength of the workers in the cane field.

Roberto's father, Melchor Clemente, was a foreman, but he worked long hours bent over in the fields with the other men for $4 a week. To support his family, the elder Clemente also managed a grocery store. Roberto developed his strong arms and large hands helping his father load and unload trucks at the store.

Melchor and Luisa Clemente always saw that their children had enough to eat. When food was scarce, Roberto's parents would wait and eat whatever was left after the children had finished.

The Clementes were a close, happy family, talking and joking together at the supper table. But they had no money for any luxuries. When Roberto was nine years old he wanted a bicycle. His father told him he would have to earn it.

Roberto found a neighbor who needed someone to carry a heavy metal milk can to the store a half mile away to be filled and brought back. Every morning before school, Roberto went for the milk. He was paid a few pennies each time, and after three long years, he had finally earned the $27 he needed to buy a used bike.

Roberto had few interests outside of his family. He was a shy, quiet, well-behaved student who seldom smiled in school. But at an early age, he fell in love with baseball.

With the hot climate in Puerto Rico, baseball can be played 12 months a year. There are winter leagues and summer leagues. As Roberto grew tall and *rangy,* he became a fast runner and spent almost every spare minute playing softball and baseball on the dirt clearings near his home.

When the boys in the neighborhood had no ball, they hit empty tin cans with a broomstick.

Roberto carried a rubber ball wherever he went and constantly squeezed it to strengthen his hands and wrists. In bed at night, he would bounce the ball against the ceiling and catch it over and over again, until his mother would tell him to quit making a racket and go to sleep. His sleep was filled with dreams of being a major league star.

One day Roberto went on an errand that took him past the big stadium in the nearby capital city of San Juan. Many major leaguers played there in the winter league, along with black players and local stars. Roberto stopped to watch the professional players and was especially impressed by a black outfielder from the mainland, Monte Irvin. Young Clemente already had a good eye: a star with the New York Giants, Irvin would eventually be *inducted* into the Baseball Hall of Fame. Roberto talked so much about his new idol that the other boys began to call him "Monte Irvin."

The softball and baseball games in which Roberto played were not organized. They were mostly informal pickup games with other boys in the neighborhood. Roberto ran awkwardly, his arms *flailing* out in every direction as he chased a ball or rounded the bases. As a hitter, he could never distinguish between a strike and a ball. He swung at everything he could reach. But he usually managed to hit the ball somewhere, even when it was pitched in the dirt or over his head. Roberto's habit of swinging at even the wildest pitches never changed throughout his career. Neither did his success as a hitter. One day he hit 10 home runs in a single sandlot game.

By the time Roberto was 14 years old, he was already playing shortstop for his high school team. He loved the game so much that he went all out on every play, running out from under his cap as he tried to be everywhere on the field at once. Win or lose, people came to the games just to watch him in action.

A man named Roberto Marín worked for the Sello Rojo Rice Company, which sponsored a local softball team. One day, Marín saw Roberto in a game and invited him to play for the company team. The older man quickly saw that Roberto's natural speed and powerful throwing arm were being wasted at shortstop, and he switched the young athlete to the outfield. The move would change Roberto's life. With lots of room to roam, Roberto soon became known for his sensational catches and his strong, accurate right arm.

From softball, Roberto graduated to baseball, playing in a local amateur league that attracted professional scouts. By the time he was 18, Clemente had improved to the point that he was ready for professional baseball, although he still had one year of high school left. Marín took the aspiring Roberto to see Pedrín Zorilla, owner of the Santurce Cangrejeros (*Crabbers*) in the Puerto Rican winter league. In addition to his activities in Puerto Rico, Zorilla also did some scouting for the Brooklyn Dodgers. The Crabbers owner did not make any promises, but he did invite Clemente to a tryout that the Dodgers were holding in San Juan.

More than 70 boys showed up for the Dodgers' tryouts. The first event was a throwing contest. After gathering together in center field, the boys were instructed to throw to home plate. Only Roberto made the catcher's mitt pop with his

At 18, Roberto was already a standout on the Santurce Crabbers, a team in the Puerto Rican winter league.

hard and true throws. Next the boys competed in the 50-yard dash, and Roberto outran them all. During batting drills, Roberto hit everything the pitcher threw, even if he had to jump in the air to reach it.

The Dodgers scout was eager to offer Roberto a contract, but major league rules prohibited any team from signing youngsters who had not yet finished high school. There was no such rule for Puerto Rican teams, however, and in the fall of 1952, Roberto signed with the Santurce Crabbers. In addition to a $400 bonus, he was paid $40 a month to play in the winter league.

Only a teenager, Roberto still had a lot to learn about playing professional baseball, and he was eager to be on the field every day. He did not understand why the manager made him sit on the bench and watch. But the winter league had many veteran players, including the great Negro League and American League pitcher Satchel Paige, and Zorilla did not want Clemente to become discouraged playing against the older, more experienced competitors. Roberto played occasionally, but he spent most of the season watching, listening, learning, and practicing.

The next season, Roberto was the regular right fielder for Santurce, playing every day. Soon major league scouts were bidding for him. Neither Roberto nor his parents could believe the amount of money that major league teams were willing to pay for the young slugger's services. The $10,000 bonus and $5,000 yearly salary offered by the Dodgers were more money than his father could earn in 20 years. Roberto accepted the offer. He was astounded a few days later when the Milwaukee Braves offered him almost three times as much. But he had given his word to the Dodgers, and he signed the contract that would take him away from his home for the first time.

As a rookie outfielder with the Montreal Royals, the Brooklyn Dodgers minor league team, Clemente spent most of his time on the bench.

3

Alone in a Strange Land

Roberto Clemente left home in the spring of 1954 with the good wishes of everyone in Puerto Rico and the determination to make them all proud of him. He knew that he was destined to be a great star. But many of the people whom Clemente later met in the Pirates organization mistook his pride for *arrogance*. A proud but inexperienced black youth who spoke a foreign language, Roberto won few friends in the Dodgers spring training camp in Florida.

On the field, however, he was electrifying. Everybody stopped to watch him play. At first glance, he appeared awkward and ungainly, but he always did everything with flare. Whether he was running the bases, swinging a bat, or throwing the ball, Roberto played every moment as if it was the most important one in his life.

Roberto was assigned to Montreal, home of the Dodgers' highest minor league team at the time. He was unhappy playing ball in Canada from the start. The weather was cold, unlike the more temperate climate of Puerto Rico. At times, the little English that he knew was useless, because many of the citizens spoke only French. And for reasons unknown to Roberto, the manager rarely let him play. Even when he did get into a game, he was often taken out for a pinch hitter if his team had a chance to score. Confused and unhappy, Roberto decided to quit and go home. But first he called his old friend, Roberto Marín, who persuaded him to stick with it and learn all that he could. If Clemente could only hold out a little longer, Marín predicted, he would soon be in the big leagues.

But Roberto was still frustrated and confused. It seemed to him that the Dodgers did not want him to do well and were trying to make him angry enough to go home.

His suspicions were probably correct. The Dodgers later admitted that they had signed Roberto just to keep their arch rivals, the New York Giants, from getting him.

The Dodgers had little need for Roberto's services because they had right fielder Carl Furillo, one of the finest defensive players in baseball. But the Giants did need a right fielder. They already had the young black superstar Willie Mays on their roster. If they added Clemente, the Giants just might be unbeatable. But the Dodgers could not hide Roberto's raw talent and drive. It was no surprise when the last-place Pittsburgh Pirates, given the first pick in the draft, announced that they were taking Clemente as their first choice.

Clemente returned to Puerto Rico for the winter season and played alongside Willie Mays and many other big leaguers for the Santurce Crabbers. The team won the Caribbean Series championship.

In 1955, finally on a team that wanted him to play, Clemente quickly became the regular right fielder with the Pirates. After a year of sitting on the bench in Montreal, he wasted little time in demonstrating his remarkable talents at bat and on the field. He made his first big league base hit in his first game against the Dodgers.

Although Roberto played well from the start, the Pirates were playing poorly as a team. With his fiery temperament, Roberto was angry and frustrated to see the team lose its first eight games of the season. He kicked and crushed and bashed the plastic batting helmets until the manager threatened to make him pay for them. He argued with umpires and even threw a punch at one of them. He was thrown out of many games. Finally, the frustration and disappointment began to take their toll on his own performance. When the season ended, he was batting only .255, a far cry from his splendid record in Puerto Rico.

From the beginning of his career, Roberto experienced very few pain-free days. In December 1954, he hurt his back in an auto accident. It bothered him off and on over the years, and more than once he considered quitting because of the discomfort. Gradually, he adapted to big league pitching. He learned to spray line drives to all fields instead of trying to hit only home runs in the spacious Forbes Field, the Pirates' home ballpark. The outfield wall at Forbes had many little turns and corners, and Roberto spent hours learning how to play the crazy bouncers that came off it.

But everyday life in Pittsburgh was difficult for Clemente. He was a stranger in a strange land, where different customs, foods, accents, and attitudes were an ongoing source of *bewilderment* for him and all his fellow Latin players.

"We Latins are people of high emotions," Roberto once told a sympathetic reporter, "and coming to this country we need time to settle down emotionally. . . . The people who never run into these problems don't have any idea at all what kind of an ordeal this can be."

The team had its spring training in Florida, a state that was still racially *segregated* in the 1950s. Black pitcher Al Jackson was a *rookie* who roomed with Clemente. "We had to live in homes with black families," Jackson recalled a number of years later. "It was galling to Roberto, who was a big star and a hero back in Puerto Rico, when he could not stay at the hotel or eat with the white players. We had to stay on the bus while they went into a restaurant. We were not part of the team except on the field."

Pittsburgh was a steel mill town with many families whose roots were in Eastern Europe, but there were few blacks and Hispanics. "People in Pittsburgh did not like [Clemente]," Roberto's teammate and future Hall of Famer Willie Stargell later wrote. "In the early '50s they weren't used to black ballplayers. Society doesn't like a proud black man, and Clemente was a proud man."

From the start of Clemente's career, the Pittsburgh sportswriters generally disliked and criticized him. "Latin players are proud," explained Stargell, "and are hurt when made fun of. Roberto's frustration was a result of unfair criticism by the media."

Roberto wanted to do well all the time, even when he was hurting so much that he could not do his best. But sometimes his injuries were too serious or too painful, and he was simply not able to play. On those occasions, the writers accused him

With the Pirates, Roberto finally got the chance to prove himself. But he still often felt that he was treated unfairly, and he frequently argued with umpires and smashed his batting helmets.

of jaking, and some players even said that he was selfish, putting his own needs before those of the team. The criticisms Roberto heard from his teammates hurt him more than all the injuries and backaches combined.

But if there were players who criticized and made fun of Roberto, there were many more who grew to respect him. Years later, Bill Virdon, a teammate and later the Pirates manager, described Clemente's development as a player and a man. "Players did not understand all he was going through coming into a strange environment," he remembered, "and they made it a little tough on him at times. . . . But I never saw a person grow more than he did."

Along with Clemente, the Pirates were also growing and improving. After years at the bottom of the league standings, the team finished second in 1958. After slipping to fourth place in 1959, the Pirates put it all together in 1960 and won the pennant by seven games. Clemente was one of the main reasons for the club's success. He batted .314, hit 14 home runs, and led the team with 94 runs batted in.

The 1960 World Series against the New York Yankees was one of the most exciting in major league history. The great Yankee *southpaw* Whitey Ford was overpowering, winning all three of his starts against the Pirates. But the Pirates held their ground and won the Series with a dramatic, ninth-inning homer in the final game. That winning home run by second baseman Bill Mazeroski in the bottom of the ninth was one of the most thrilling moments in any World Series.

Understandably, Mazeroski's heroic performance was the center of everyone's attention, overshadowing Clemente's consistently fine play. The Pirates slugger hit safely in all seven games of the Series, with nine hits overall and a .310 batting average.

After Mazeroski's Series-winning blast, the Pirates celebrated wildly in the clubhouse. Amid all the excitement, some of the sportswriters no-ticed that Clemente was not there with his team-mates. They wondered aloud—and later in print—why he would abandon the rest of his team on such a glorious occasion.

Where was Roberto? Still in uniform, he had stepped outside the clubhouse door and into the stadium walkway. He wanted to share the moment with the fans, the people who cheered for him and who paid his salary. While the rest of the team was inside the clubhouse whooping it up, Clemente was outside in the stadium, shaking hands and signing autographs.

Since joining the Pirates, Clemente had often spoken out publicly against his treatment by the sportswriters in Pittsburgh. Over the years, his poor relationship with the media had begun to take its toll, and now the Pirates right fielder was all but ignored by the journalists when it came to handing out the credit for the team's success.

As everyone expected, Pirate Dick Groat was chosen as the National League's Most

Valuable Player. An excellent shortstop, Groat won the batting title with a .325 average. Clemente—who batted .314 and was named the league's outstanding right fielder—was a distant eighth in the balloting for Most Valuable Player.

Back home in Puerto Rico for the winter, Roberto brooded over what he considered an insult by the press, which selects the Most Valuable Player. He felt that he had played exceptionally well during the 1960 season and had not gotten the credit that he deserved from the sportswriters. To make things worse, Roberto voiced his displeasure to anyone who would listen, including journalists. Soon, he had created even more enemies among the media. But Roberto felt betrayed by the sportswriters in Pittsburgh and around the country, and he stopped caring what they thought or said about him. He was so bitter, in fact, that for years he did not wear his World Series ring.

Although he was always popular with the fans, Clemente never felt he received the respect that he deserved from the sportswriters. They often criticized him for showing off on the field or complaining about his injuries.

4

"The Most Exciting Player I Ever Saw"

During the next five years, Clemente developed into the *premier* right fielder in baseball. In addition to his consistently outstanding defensive play, he won three batting titles during the stretch and was named to the All-Star team each year. But in spite of his fine performance, the Pirates failed to repeat as world champions, finishing no higher than third place during the five-year period.

Predictably, the Pittsburgh writers and broadcasters blamed Roberto for the team's problems, continuing a negative media campaign against him. Things were not much better in the national media, where all the attention was focused on sluggers Mickey Mantle of the New York Yankees, Willie Mays of the San Francisco Giants, and Henry Aaron of the Milwaukee Braves.

But the players knew better. As most of them agreed, Clemente could win a game in more ways than anyone else in baseball—with his bat, with his tireless hustling, with his strong throwing arm, and with his superb intelligence on the field. Perhaps his greatest achievements were as a fielder. In recognition of his outstanding defensive play, Roberto's fellow players would award him the Gold Glove Award as the league's best right fielder for 12 years in a row.

He was also a dangerous batter. A *notorious* bad-ball hitter, Roberto had few weaknesses at the plate, a fact that put fear into the hearts of pitchers around the league. "He would hit pitches thrown over his head, down by his ankles, inside, outside," remembered the great Dodgers pitcher Johnny Podres. "I'd get two quick strikes on him and never get the third one. No matter where I threw it, he'd hit it."

According to Podres, Roberto was also a dedicated team player, in spite of the unflattering picture painted by the press. "If a double was needed," Podres insisted, "he would go for that. If there were two out and the Pirates needed a run, he would go for the home run. But he would not swing for the fences if his team was down by 3 or 4 runs. He would just try to get on base. That's a team player."

Rookies in the league learned quickly to respect Clemente's powerful right arm. But sometimes they had to learn the hard way, as catcher Joe Torre did when he broke in with the Milwaukee Braves in 1961. "I got a hit to right field and rounded first base as most runners do," remembered Torre years later. "Clemente picked up the ball, faked a throw to second and threw it so fast behind me to first base I was caught and tagged out. It was my most embarrassing moment on the field."

The ability to anticipate what would happen next, to think ahead of the other player, was the key to Clemente's game. "He was a complete player," said Pirates coach Alex Grammas, "thinking all the time."

Late in his career, pitcher Nelson Briles was traded from the St. Louis Cardinals to the Pirates. Shortly after joining the Pirates, the former Cardinals star learned an embarrassing lesson about questioning Clemente's judgment on the field. Briles admitted, "I never gave him credit for his ability until I was on the same team."

"One day I was pitching," remembered Briles, "and Willie McCovey, a lefthand pull hitter, was at bat. Clemente was not playing him to pull, so I waved Robby a few steps closer to the right field line. I was ready to pitch and I glanced out there at him and he had moved back. So I waved him over again and he took a few steps toward the line. I pitched and McCovey hit a screaming line drive into the right center field gap. I knew it was good for a double and I ran over to back up third base. When I got there, I discovered that Clemente had caught the ball."

Back in the dugout, Clemente made sure that Briles had gotten the message. "I bet you, Nellie," he laughed self-confidently, "you no figure out how I made that catch. It is because the great Roberto knows how to play the hitter and the pitcher each day. You were pitching good and I knew that hitter could not pull the ball on you, so I move back after you move me. Nellie, you never have to check the great Roberto."

After years of playing together, Clemente and the superb Pirate second baseman Bill Mazeroski were a flawless duo on the field, working out a number of special plays to fool base runners. One play was particularly popular with the fans—and irritating to opposing players. With a runner on second base, Mazeroski would sometimes let a hard-hit ground ball go right past him, only to be scooped up by the speeding Clemente who would throw the runner out at first base. They reasoned that the right-fielder, with his exceptional throwing arm, had a better chance than the second baseman of nailing the runner at first.

"Nobody in the National League," insisted Clemente's manager Bill Virdon, "had an arm like his, for strength and accuracy." All-Star center fielder Richie Ashburn, for years one of the finest players in the league, agreed. Years later, working as a sports announcer, Ashburn was outspoken in his praise of Clemente: "He was the best right fielder I ever saw in 40 years."

But Ashburn was not the only player or manager to single out Roberto's performance. "Clemente was the best player I competed against and the most exciting I ever saw," declared Dodgers ace Don Sutton after his retirement. A Hall of Fame pitcher who won 324 games over a span of 23 seasons, Sutton had seen plenty of other great players with whom to compare Roberto.

Clemente never failed to give an autograph to a fan. "I believe I owe something to the people who watch us," he told one sportswriter. "They work hard for their money."

Many other old timers felt the same way. Sparky Anderson, who managed both the Cincinnati Reds and the Detroit Tigers to world championships, was similarly enthusiastic in his praise of Clemente. "In my 22 years as a manager," Anderson recalled, "I never saw a better player than Roberto Clemente. No player at any position could do anything better than he did it."

With his powerful right arm, Clemente was the terror of base runners leaguewide. On the base paths himself, however, Roberto had little fear of opposing outfielders.

Teammate Al Jackson later recalled what an intimidating presence Clemente was as a base runner. "He was the only player I ever saw," Jackson remembered, "who would hit a single to left field and round first so hard he would get halfway to second, and have to hit the dirt and slide to stop himself, then pop up and get back to first base. If the left fielder bobbled the ball, [Roberto] would be into second easily, but he always got back to first if he had to. He played that hard and intensely all the time."

Playing with such drive and intensity every day gradually began to take its toll on Clemente's already ailing body. The sudden stops, starts, turns, and slides and the jarring contact with outfield walls and catchers blocking home plate left him battered and weary at the end of the day. Because of this, Clemente valued his rest and his privacy and seldom went out with his teammates after a game.

Other players took the winters off after they had established themselves in the big leagues. But Roberto realized that his fellow Puerto Ricans had little chance to see him perform for the Pirates, and every year he played the winter season in the Puerto Rican league instead of resting.

One day in the winter of 1963, Clemente noticed an attractive young woman in a store near his home. He fell in love at once and knew that he wanted to marry her. The young woman's name was Vera Zabala, and Roberto wasted no time trying to get to know her. According to local customs, however, she could not speak to him directly until they had been properly introduced. And even after that, she would not go out on a date with him without a chaperon. Almost a year later, on November 14, 1964, Roberto and Vera were married. With Roberto's major league salary, the newlyweds were able to move into a new house on a hill looking out over the ocean.

In the years that followed, they had three sons: Roberto, Jr., Luis, and Enrique. Roberto soon became a devoted family man. At home in Puerto Rico, he learned to make ceramics and driftwood sculptures. He also loved to travel with his family throughout Central America. The country he most loved to visit was Nicaragua.

Each summer, Clemente's family moved with him to Pittsburgh, where Vera went to school to learn English. Little by little, Roberto mellowed on the field. He still argued calls that he thought an umpire had missed, but he did not get thrown out of as many games as before. He realized that he could not be much help to his team if he was in the shower. Now a matured veteran and one of the older players in the league, Clemente emerged as the Pirates leader.

Pictured here with fellow superstars Willie Mays (center) and Henry Aaron (right), Clemente often felt that his accomplishments were unfairly overshadowed by the attention paid to the other two.

5

Clemente the Comedian and Much More

There was another side to Bobby Clemente—as most of the league's players had begun to call him—that the public rarely saw. Not only was he the league's most intense and determined athlete, he was also one of the biggest jokesters and story-tellers in the clubhouse.

"Clemente was the funniest man I ever saw in a clubhouse," Tony Bartirome, the Pirates trainer, fondly remembered, "but only among the players. He had the knack of getting a team up, if they were in a slump, by making everybody relax and feel good. He was at the center of the noise and life and laughter in the clubhouse, but as soon as the writers came in, he clammed up. They never saw it."

Pirates manager Bill Virdon agreed, "You got him going on a plane or bus telling jokes and stories and he had everybody in stitches."

Clemente also loved to talk about his life outside of baseball. He was proud of his six months of military service in the Marine reserves. When anyone in the clubhouse asked him about it, he would be on stage for at least an hour describing his experiences in vivid detail.

He also loved to hear the humorous story of a clubhouse prank involving a life-size wax statue of him that stood in the Pirates front office. One day, Bartirome carried the statue of Clemente into the clubhouse.

"I took it into an empty room adjacent to the clubhouse," the Pirates trainer later recalled. "It was dark and cold in there. I laid it on a platform and covered it to the chin with a blanket while some of the players watched. Then I called the team doctor and told him, 'Bobby's real sick, doc, you better do something. We put him in the side room in case the writers came in.'"

As Bartirome remembered it years later, the clubhouse was dark and shadowy, the only light filtering in from a nearby bathroom. The doctor touched the statue's hand; it was as cold as ice. Concerned, he put his ear to the statue's chest to check for a heartbeat. He heard nothing.

"My God," cried the team physician as he raised his head from the wax body, "he's dead!" By this time, everyone in the entire clubhouse was roaring with laughter.

In addition to his sense of humor, Clemente was also one of the kindest and most considerate men in the league. He would go out of his way to speak with the wives and children of ballpark employees whenever he saw them. And he was always ready to do a favor for a teammate.

Richie Ashburn later recalled one typical incident on a snowy night in Pittsburgh. "Bobby and I were at one of those winter banquets," Ashburn related, "and the snow was deep on the roads. After it was over he offered to drive me to the airport. I figured it was on his way, or he was going there, too, so I said okay. I found out later that he was really going to the other side of the city and it was far out of his way."

In spite of his outspoken pride in his abilities, Clemente never acted as if his skills on the field made him any better than anyone else. In spring training, he bunked with the young players at Pirate City in Bradenton, Florida, while the other regulars stayed in condominiums on the beach. He knew the young players needed help adjusting, especially the Latins—just as he had needed help years earlier. He talked with the young players at night, cheered them up and encouraged them when they made mistakes.

"I know what you're going through," he would tell the rookies, "because I've been through it myself."

In Pittsburgh, the established players were in great demand to speak at lunches and banquets. The stars could pick up $500 or more for a single appearance, but the lesser-known regulars and the bench warmers were seldom invited. One day Clemente called a club meeting. He proposed that all speaking fees be pooled together and divided evenly among all the players, including those who were never asked to speak. But one of the other Pirates stars refused to go along with the proposal, and Clemente's goal was never realized. Roberto did put his plan into practice on a smaller scale, however. In the future, he agreed to speak only if a lesser-known player was also invited to accompany him. The two of them then split the total fee fifty-fifty.

On one occasion, Clemente agreed to appear in a television commercial for a big fee. Other players were hired at a much lower rate to stand in the background. Roberto discovered this and demanded that the others receive the same amount as he was earning. When the sponsor refused, Roberto turned down the job.

In 1966, Clemente finally achieved the recognition that he had always believed he deserved. He was named the National League's Most Valuable Player, even though the Pirates finished in third place. Roberto was sensational from opening day to the end of the season, hitting .317 with career highs in home runs (29) and runs batted in (119). He was the first player from Puerto Rico ever to win the award.

"This makes me happy," Roberto said when he received the award, "because now the people feel that if I could do it, then maybe they could do it. The kids have someone to look up to and to follow."

The next year, Clemente won his fourth and last batting title with a .357 average, driving in 100 runs. But once again, the Pirates were not up to his standards, and the team skidded to a distant sixth place in the league.

As he got older, Clemente developed *arthritis* in his neck and shoulders. Before the 1968 season, he fell and hurt his shoulder, badly aggravating the problems that he had experienced throughout his career. Seeking whatever relief he could find during the team's long road trips, he went to a *chiropractor* on several occasions and even tried a *hypnotist* one winter in Puerto Rico.

In 1967, Roberto became the first Pirates player to earn $100,000. Because of his leadership on the field and in the clubhouse, his teammates picked him to be their player representative. But even after this, he still got little respect from the media, which continued to criticize him for being selfish and uncooperative. "The only people who criticize me are writers," answered Clemente when one journalist still had the *audacity* to accuse him of not being a team player.

By now, as far as the fans were concerned, Roberto was the greatest. They loved his all-out style of play and the fact that, unlike many other stars of his stature, he never failed to sign an autograph. "I feel proud when a kid asks me for my autograph," he explained. "I believe I owe something to the people who watch us. They work hard for their money."

"He spoke to me about personal pride..." remembered teammate Willie Stargell. "There was nothing that made Roberto prouder than being a major leaguer. One could see it in the way he dressed and carried himself."

In 1967, Clemente won his fourth and final National League batting title with a .357 average, but the Pirates stumbled to sixth place in the league.

"Robby led by example," said teammate Richie Hebner. "When he was 36, if he hit a tap back to the pitcher, he still roared down to first base like the cops were chasing him. When we young players saw that, we told ourselves if he's bearing down like that after 16 years in the majors, we'd better do that, too, or we'll look bad."

Under Roberto's leadership and with a blend of veteran and younger players, the Pirates climbed back on top of the National League East in 1970. At 36 years of age, Clemente batted a spectacular .352 that season.

On July 16, 1970, Clemente received one of the biggest thrills of his career. At the opening of Pittsburgh's new Three Rivers Stadium, the Pirates fans and teammates honored him in a special evening ceremony. Among the gifts Roberto received was a scroll with the names of more than 300,000 Puerto Rican well-wishers.

Age and injury began to catch up with Clemente during his later years in the league. But he always played with the same drive and intensity, even when he was in pain.

CHAPTER

6

A Hero's
Death

At the age of 37, Roberto Clemente in some ways seemed to have the body of a 21-year-old. But with all the aches and bruises he had collected over the years, he felt at times as if he was 100.

At 5 feet, 11 inches tall, he still weighed a firm 183 pounds—all muscle, no fat. But when he swung a bat, he sometimes grabbed his neck and grimaced with pain. He missed almost 50 games in 1970 and 20 games in the Pirates' championship season of 1971.

In the spring of 1972, Clemente announced that he would play baseball for only two more years. Ankle injuries and bruised heels had slowed him down too much. Stomach problems caused him to lose weight, and he missed 47 of the first 116 games, including the All-Star game, to which he had been named for the twelfth time.

Roberto had played hard for his entire career. He had given everything he had every day for 18 years, and he was finally running out of energy. As the 1972 season wore on, the Pirates built a sizeable lead in the National League East, and Roberto could afford to rest more often. After all, he had already collected more hits and driven in more runs than anybody who had ever played for the Pirates, a team that had once been the home of such great hitters as Hall of Famers Honus Wagner and Pie Traynor. Roberto, however, was rapidly closing in on another goal.

Of all the thousands of men who had played major league baseball, only 10—all of them now

Hall of Famers—had ever collected 3,000 base hits. By the end of August 1972, Clemente needed only 25 hits to reach this rare plateau. Years earlier, Hall of Famer Lou Boudreau had called Clemente "the worst looking great hitter I've ever seen." And at 37, Roberto still did everything wrong. He twisted his head when he stepped to the plate, jumped around in the batter's box, and swung at pitches far out of the strike zone. But in spite of his unconventional style as a hitter, Roberto was about to achieve one of the most difficult batting goals in all of baseball.

Throughout September, Clemente piled up the hits. On September 28, the calculator reached 2,999. The next night in Pittsburgh, Roberto faced the Mets ace and future Hall of Famer Tom Seaver. In the first inning, Roberto swung down on a pitch and hit a high bouncer that the second baseman managed to reach with his glove but could not hold. At first the crowd went wild, as the ball trickled into right field and the "hit" sign was flashed on the scoreboard. But the cheers quickly changed to boos. The scoreboard operator had misunderstood the call and now the "error" sign was displayed.

With Seaver on the mound, Clemente went hitless the rest of the night. At first he was angry and disappointed at the ruling. But after thinking it over, he decided that he would rather reach his goal with a clean hit, not one that might be questioned. The next day he did just that, smashing a hard line drive off the wall for a double. The game was stopped while the Mets outfielder threw the ball to shortstop Jim Fregosi. Fregosi then handed the ball to umpire Doug Harvey, who presented it to Clemente.

"Congratulations, Roberto," Harvey said as he handed Clemente the ball.

"Great achievement," added Fregosi.

Clemente thanked them, smiling broadly at the crowd. Willie Mays, who had already reached the 3,000-hit mark a couple of years before, ran out of the Mets dugout to shake Roberto's hand.

For once, Roberto was clearly feeling no pain. After the game, he dedicated the hit to the fans of Pittsburgh and the people of Puerto Rico, especially his old friend, Roberto Marín.

In the five-game championship series against Cincinnati, Clemente had only four hits. This time, the Pirates lost, three games to two. With the season over and his goal finally achieved, Roberto was exhausted and ready to go home to Puerto Rico.

Clemente was the first major league superstar from Puerto Rico, and he took the role seriously. He wanted to show that other youngsters from the Caribbean Islands could make it to the top. For several years, he had worked to build a sports center in San Juan, with baseball fields, basketball and tennis courts, a swimming pool,

Clemente collected his 3,000th hit on September 30, 1972. At the time, he was only the 11th player to reach that milestone.

and dormitories. Clemente planned for it to be open to everyone at no cost.

Christmas and New Year's Eve are very festive holidays in Puerto Rico. There are parties and fiestas everywhere. In 1972, the happy mood was interrupted on the day before Christmas Eve by the news from Nicaragua that a severe earthquake had destroyed much of the capital city of Managua, killing 10,000 people and leaving 200,000 homeless. Hearing the news, Clemente immediately cancelled all of his holiday plans and began working to collect money, food, and other supplies for the stricken people. As chairman of the island's Nicaraguan relief effort, he worked day and night, eating little and resting even less. In one week alone, workers collected enough food and supplies to fill a cargo plane that would fly across the Caribbean Sea to Nicaragua.

Clemente did not like to fly, and at first he did not plan to accompany the relief workers on the airplane. But he heard rumors that General

Somoza, the Nicaraguan dictator, was stealing some of the donated food and money for his army and selling the rest to the homeless victims. Roberto believed that Somoza's soldiers would be afraid to steal the supplies if a prominent person was on the scene to watch them. "I'll go down and distribute the supplies myself," he told reporters shortly before leaving Puerto Rico.

Soon after 9:00 on the night of December 31, 1972, the plane bearing Clemente and the other relief workers took off. A few minutes later, the plane's engines faltered. At once, the plane lost speed, made a sharp left turn, and fell into the Caribbean Sea. Everyone onboard was killed.

Despite a steady rain, thousands of people lined the beach on the morning of New Year's Day 1973, hoping against hope for a miracle: that their hero might be found still alive, or at least that his body might be found. But there was no miracle.

Pirates slugger Willie Stargell "cried like a baby" when he heard the news.

"He died a terribly misunderstood individual," Stargell later wrote. "His teammates loved and respected him. . . . Only in his final year did he begin to get the respect and admiration he deserved. . . . After blasting him for 17 years, the papers all extolled him."

In the week following Clemente's death, a huge, lighted display board on a mountaintop overlooking the city of Pittsburgh carried the message, *"Adiós, Amigo Roberto,"* which means, "Good-bye, friend Roberto."

The Pirates chartered a plane to take them to Puerto Rico for the funeral. Many other players flew in to join Roberto's family and friends at the graveside. A special memorial service was also held in Pittsburgh.

A fierce and determined competitor, Clemente always craved the recognition of the fans and his fellow players. But it was left to his widow Vera to collect the numerous honors and awards that followed his untimely death.

A few months later, the Hall of Fame Induction Committee waived its five-year waiting rule and inducted Clemente into the prestigious club. In the spring, the Pirates wore a small round patch on their sleeves bearing the number 21, the number on Roberto's uniform throughout his career with the Pirates. The number was officially retired by the team on April 6, 1973. Thirteen years later, Ruben Sierra, a young major league star who had learned to play baseball at Roberto's Sports City in San Juan, proudly began wearing the number 21 on his Texas Rangers uniform.

The Pittsburgh Pirates missed their leader on the field. The fans missed Clemente's electrifying grace and ferocious flare. But for all his glorious achievements on the diamond, Roberto Clemente was best remembered simply as a man. As his friend Willie Stargell put it, "It's the goodness in that man that I miss."

Further Reading

Brondfield, Jerry. *Roberto Clemente: Pride of the Pirates.* Champaign, IL: Garrard, 1976.

Christine, Bill. *Roberto!* New York: Stadia Sports, 1973.

Gerber, Irving. *Roberto Clemente: The Pride of Puerto Rico.* North Bergen, NJ: Book-Lab, 1978.

Miller, Ira, and Jose M. Perez. *Roberto Clemente.* New York: Grosset & Dunlap, 1973.

Musick, Phil. *Who Was Roberto?* Garden City, NY: Doubleday, 1974.

Glossary

agenda   a plan of things to be considered or done

arrogance   a feeling of being too proud of oneself; conceited

arthritis   a painful irritation and swelling of the joints of the body

audacity   rude or disrespectful behavior; also, courageous and bold behavior

bewilderment   the state of being greatly puzzled

chiropractor   a doctor who adjusts the body's structures, such as the spinal column, for proper alignment or positioning

crabber   one who fishes for crabs

flail   to move or swing wildly

hypnotist   a person who puts someone into a relaxed, sleeplike, but alert trance known as hypnosis

induct   to admit as a member

notorious   being well known for something bad or unpleasant

premier   the first in position, rank, or importance

rangy   having long limbs; tall and slim

rookie   a first-year member of a team

segregated   separated from others or from a group, sometimes based on skin color

southpaw   a left-handed baseball pitcher

strike   a ball pitched in the strike zone, swung at and missed, or not hit fair; also a perfectly thrown ball

underdog   a person or group that is expected to lose a contest or struggle

Chronology

1934   Born Roberto Walker Clemente on August 18 in Carolina, Puerto Rico

1947   Jackie Robinson joins the Brooklyn Dodgers and becomes the first black player in the major leagues

1948   Discovered by scout Roberto Marín

1952   Signs first professional contract with the Santurce Cangrejeros of the Puerto Rican League

1954   Signed by the Brooklyn Dodgers in February and assigned to Triple-A Montreal Royals; purchased by the Pittsburgh Pirates in November for $4,000 draft price

1955   In April, Clemente singles against Brooklyn in first major league at-bat

1960   Pirates win World Series in seven games over the New York Yankees

1961   Records 1,000th career base hit; wins
first batting title with .351 average;
wins first of 12 Gold Gloves Awards;
appears in first All-Star Game

1964   Marries Vera Cristina Zabala; wins
second batting title

1965   Wins third batting title

1966   Records 2,000th base hit; becomes first
Puerto Rican baseball player to win the
MVP Award

1967   Wins fourth and final batting title with
a .357 average

1970   Honored at Three Rivers Stadium in
Pittsburgh with Roberto Clemente Night

1971   Bats .414 in World Series against the Baltimore Orioles and is named Series MVP

1972   Records 3,000th base hit; killed in
plane crash on New Year's Eve

1973   Clemente's number 21 is retired by the
Pirates; becomes the first Hispanic player
to be voted into the Hall of Fame

Index

78

Norman L. Macht holds a bachelor of philosophy degree from the University of Chicago and a master's degree in political science from Sonoma State University. He writes extensively on finance and sports history and has written several biographies for the Chelsea House BASEBALL LEGENDS series. Macht is also the author of *Christopher Columbus, Sojourner Truth, Sandra Day O'Connor,* and *Muhammad Ali* in the Chelsea House JUNIOR WORLD BIOGRAPHIES series.

Picture Credits